Higher Ground

Inspiration to Take You to the Top

Ron & Ryan Sutton

Unless otherwise indicated, all Scripture quotations are taken from the King James Version (KJV) of the Bible.

ABOUT THE AUTHORS

Ron Sutton was converted during the Jesus Movement in 1972. His ministry has taken him to sixty nations. He has conducted mass crusades and leaders' conferences, served as a missionary, evangelist, pastor and church planter. His books on evangelism, gospel tracts and pro-life literature have been distributed throughout the USA and internationally. He and his wife Cindy established a drug rehabilitation ministry, a childrens' home in Costa Rica, and a home for unwed mothers. Ron served as director of the School of Christ International in Africa. He is currently planting a church near St. Louis, while continuing to travel in ministry, and assist his son Ryan at The Grace Center.

Ryan Sutton surrendered to the call to preach under the ministry of B.H. Clendennen a few days after his fourteenth birthday in 1997. He preached his first sermon the following Sunday and was ordained to pastor his first church three years later. He has preached in churches and revivals throughout the

USA and has ministered internationally in China, Russia, India, Europe, Africa and Latin America. Ryan continues to travel and preach throughout the nation while serving as the senior pastor of The Grace Center, a dynamic multi-cultural church, in Festus, Missouri.

TO ORDER MATERIALS OR SCHEDULE MEETINGS

The Grace Center

P.O. Box 21, Crystal City, Missouri 63019

636-465-0885

www.TheGraceCenter.com | www.RyanSutton.org

CONTENTS

1

Winning in Life

To win in life we must proceed with purpose.

"I press toward the goal for the prize of the upward call of God in Christ Jesus" (Philippians 3:14).

It requires patience and perseverance to endure difficulty and to overcome obstacles encountered in pursuit of a goal.

The devil's design is to discourage you and steal your vision—to get your eyes off the goal. He wants to bring you to the place where you are just going through the motions, doing just enough to get by. He wants you to focus your energy on surviving, rather than on winning. But for the Christian, survival is not an acceptable goal.

We must expect God to help us do more than survive. He has not called us to be survivors. He has called us to be winners. Not all survivors are winners but all winners are survivors. God will help us become winners.

"In all these things we are more than conquerors through Him who loved us" (Romans 8:37).

Plan to win. God is on your side.

"Fear not, for I am with you; be not dismayed, for I am your God. I will strengthen you, yes I will help you, I will uphold you with My righteous right hand" (Isaiah 41:10).

2

Turning Troubles into Triumphs

"Many are the afflictions of the righteous, but the Lord delivers him out of them all" (Psalm 34:19).

The people of God are not strangers to trouble. The faithful followers of Jesus are well acquainted with the hard places on the highway of faith. Successes are often followed by setbacks, victories by defeat.

But the setbacks and defeats are temporary. We are destined for victory and success. We should not be discouraged by trouble. Faith doesn't save us from trouble. But it will save us from defeat. Faith enables us to tenaciously hold to God through the valley, the storm, the trouble and trial. And eventually it has a way of reversing trouble and failure.

Joseph is the best example I know of someone who turned troubles into triumphs by faith. His adversities became advances. His setbacks didn't stop him. We need to learn from him: whether we triumph over trouble or surrender to it, depends not on the degree or duration of our troubles, but on the way we respond to them.

Troubles are temporary. Triumph in Christ is eternal. Faith will not fail you. It has the power to squeeze triumph out of trouble.

"But as for you, you meant evil against me; but God meant it for good, in order to bring it about as it is this day, to save many people alive" (Genesis 50:20).

3

Dealing with Disappointment

It's not unusual to experience disappointment from time to time. It might come from feelings of loneliness or rejection, or from not receiving a gift desired. The important thing is to deal with disappointment and not allow it to deteriorate into depression.

The key in dealing with it is to face it. Don't deny it. It's OK to be disappointed, as long as you recover from it!

How do you recover? First by reminding yourself that God, not people or things, is the ultimate source of happiness. If you try to deal with disappointment by escaping into television, by over eating, spending money you don't have on things you don't need, etc. you are setting yourself up for depression. If you deal with disappointment by pouring your heart out to God, by seeking His face, by looking for help in His word, you will find joy and strength.

Disappointment can be your friend, if you let it drive you deeper into God.

"Praise be to the Lord, for He has heard my cry for mercy. The Lord is my strength and shield; my heart trusts in Him and I am helped..." (Psalm 28:6-7).

"Be of good courage, and He shall strengthen your heart, all you that hope in the Lord" (Psalm 30:24).

4

Don't Quit

The following poem has blessed me time and time again for many years. I hope you will find it encouraging as I have.

"When things go wrong as they
sometimes will,
When the road you're treading
seems all up hill,
When the funds are low and the debts are high
And you want to smile, but you have to sigh,
When care is pressing you down a bit,
Rest if you must, but don't you quit.
Life is strange with its twists and turns
As every one of us sometimes learns
And many a failure turns about
When he might have won had he stuck it out;

15

Don't give up though the pace seems slow—

You may succeed with another blow.

Success is failure turned inside out—

The silver tint of the clouds of doubt,

And you never can tell just how close you are,

It may be near when it seems so far;

So stick to the fight when you're hardest hit—

It's when things seem worst that

you must not quit."

5

Passing Through

"Blessed is the man who endures temptation; for when he has been proved, he will receive the crown of life which the Lord has promised to those who love him" (James 1:12).

"God does not offer us a way out of the testings of life. He offers us a way through." W.T. Purkiser

It is a futile exercise to attempt to avoid the trials of life. Wisdom teaches us to meet them without worry and pass through them in faith.

Faith does not grow, we do not become stronger, on the easy path. Our strength increases and our faith grows by overcoming obstacles, not by avoiding them.

It is not work, but worry which robs us of faith and strength. Worrying about obstacles will weaken and defeat you. Worry will rob you of peace and break down your faith. Working in faith to overcome obstacles will strengthen you and increase your faith. Worry is the fruit of unbelief. It will rob you of energy. It will waste your strength. It will leave you confused and helpless before the smallest trial.

Faith is the way to travel. Faith doesn't worry when it meets an obstacle; it rolls up its sleeves and goes to work to conquer it. There is no easy way out. In fact, there is only one way out for you: through. It's time to stop waiting for God to get you out. It's time to put your faith to work and go through.

You can do it! God is with you.

"Beloved, do not think it strange concerning the fiery trial which is to try you, as though some strange thing happened to you; but rejoice to the extent that you partake of Christ's sufferings, that when His glory is revealed, you may also be glad with exceeding joy" (I Peter 4:12-13).

6

Don't Ever Give Up

"These things I have spoken to you, that in Me you may have peace. In the world you will have tribulation; but be of good cheer, I have overcome the world" (John 16:33).

The devil does all he can to discourage and defeat you. He knows that he can't win if you refuse to quit. You may feel that life has served you more than your fair share of discouragement and disappointment. But don't lose heart. God's intention is to help, strengthen, and bless you. Discouragement and disappointment will pass. They are temporary. You are destined to eternally enjoy the goodness and the glory of God.

In times of discouragement, we tend to look at the circumstances. The more we look, the more discouraged we become. Faith will help us turn away from temporary, negative circumstances to look to God. The key to victory is always to look away then look up. After we have our eyes fixed on God, we get in a position to hear His voice. Our faith is strengthened as we spend time in His presence and hear His Word. Then we can face the circumstances, which once threatened to overcome us, with an attitude of faith and victory.

God is with you. God is for you. You will win, if you don't quit.

"Therefore we also, since we are surrounded by so great a cloud of witnesses, let us lay

aside every weight, and the sin which so easily ensnares us, and let us run with endurance the race that is set before us, looking unto Jesus, the author and finisher of our faith, who for the joy that was set before Him endured the cross, despising the shame, and has sat down at the right hand of the throne of God" (Hebrews 12:1-2).

7

The Sun Will Rise Again

"Who redeems your life from destruction, who crowns you with lovingkindness and tender mercies" (Psalms 103:4).

Has a period of darkness left you discouraged? Has it lasted too long? Are you wondering if things are ever going to change? Do you hear voices in the darkness that are often not God's voice? Do you hear thoughts in your head that say, "It's over. All hope is gone?" Those aren't God's thoughts. They are not even your thoughts. They are lies of the devil. He is a master counterfeiter. He makes his thoughts sound like your thoughts. The devil is a liar. God is going to bring you through this thing. It's bigger than you are, and God knows that you need His help. You have done everything you can do but the darkness hasn't lifted and the winds are still blowing. The ship of your life is being shattered and you feel helpless to stop it. What can you do? You can do what Paul did: Trust God, listen for His voice and, when you hear it, speak by faith into the darkness. You are going to get through this by believing, speaking and acting on the Word of God.

Sometimes there aren't any explanations for what you are going through. It is difficult to bear the pain; it is more difficult to make any sense out of it. All you can do is lift up your hands, praise Him like Paul did, and say, "I trust You. I don't understand but I trust You. It doesn't make any sense but I trust You." There will be victories after the valleys of life but the ultimate victory will be experienced in the next. Faith will help you to remember that even if life

on earth is filled with long periods of pain,
Heaven is on the other side of it.

8

It's Not Over at the End of Your Rope

Have you ever heard a preacher say, "When you get to the end of your rope, tie a knot and hang on until God comes to help."

There are times when all you can do is hang on. But there are also times when it's best to let go. Sometimes at the end of yourself you find God waiting to catch you.

"The eternal God is your refuge, and underneath are the everlasting arms; He will thrust out the enemy from before you, and will say, 'Destroy!'" (Deuteronomy 33:27).

God expects effort from us. He expects us to use the ability and the energy He gives us. But when we fail, He doesn't leave us on our own. He is standing by, ready to help when we call out to Him in faith.

Jesus said we could come to Him and find rest for our weary souls. He also said we could get yoked up with Him. To be "yoked up" implies walking side-by-side. In the process of walking with Him we learn how to live a victorious life.

Sometimes the way to victory is not hanging on, but letting go. When you get to the end of your rope it's time to trust Jesus, to call out to Him in faith, to draw near to Him. It's time to respond to His invitation in Matthew 11:28–29:

"Come to Me, all you who labor and are heavy laden, and I will give you rest. Take My yoke

upon you and learn from Me, for I am gentle and lowly in heart, and you will find rest for your souls" (Matthew 11:28-29).

9

Water in the Wilderness

Exodus 17 tells the story of the children of Israel at Rephidim—a dry place. When faced with the need for water they immediately began to murmur. They doubted God. They didn't remember all the times God had miraculously met their needs.

God, in His mercy, met their need for water— even though they didn't reach out to Him in faith. Moses smote the rock in obedience to the word of the Lord and water flowed out. We know from 1 Corinthians 10:4 that the rock was a type of Christ, who was smitten on the cross resulting in living water for those who believe on Him.

God warns us to understand a few things about the dry places. First, it is normal to pass through a dry place now and then. Secondly, God can meet your need in the dry place. Thirdly, it is important to trust God while experiencing spiritual dryness. Don't murmur and doubt as the children of Israel did. Remember, God is your source. His supplies are unlimited. If necessary, He can bring water out of the rock—or even make it out of nothing.

You will get through the dry place—and when you do you will have an even greater appreciation for the water of life.

"Whoever drinks of the water that I shall give him will never thirst. But the water that I shall give him will become in him a fountain of

water springing up into everlasting life" (John 4:14).

10

Walking by Faith

I will never forget a short message preached in Costa Rica by my friend Tino Wallenda—from the high wire! Thousands of eyes were riveted on him as he walked, danced, jumped and skipped rope on the wire. There was absolute silence as he spoke through a wireless microphone on the subject "Walking by Faith."

Tino explained that walking the high wire is a lot like walking by faith. One of the things he does to maintain balance is to pick out a certain point at the other end of the wire and focus his vision and attention on that point. That's what Hebrews 12 tells us to do in order to live a balanced Christian life. *"Looking unto Jesus the author and finisher of our faith..."*

(Hebrews 12:2). The Amplified Bible says it like this: *"Looking away (from all that will distract) to Jesus…"*

The distractions are the things that cause us to lose focus—to get off track. They are the weights and sin, mentioned in verse one, which trip us up and get us off balance.

Are you beset by distracting trials and temptation? Are you discouraged? Do you feel like you have lost your balance and that you are about to fall? Don't give up! You can make it if you will persist and walk by faith. It's time to refocus and regain your spiritual balance by "looking unto Jesus, the author and finisher of your faith."

11

The Blessed Believer

Psalm 1:1-3

His Path—three things he avoids (v. 1)

- The counsel of the ungodly
- The path of sinners
- Fellowship with the scornful

His Pleasure (v. 2)

- His delight is in God's Word

His Position (v. 3)

- Strongly rooted in God, like a tree planted by the river

His Productivity (v. 3)

- Bears fruit and prospers

In contrast, the ungodly are compared to "chaff which the wind drives away." One does well to remember that the apparent prosperity of the ungodly is a temporary, fleeting thing. It will be quickly blown away. They have no root, no enduring substance, no strength to stand.

The truly prosperous person is the one who is rooted in God—who loves to learn and delights to do God's word.

"But his delight is in the law of the Lord, and in His law he meditates day and night" (vs. 2)

12

Persevering in Faith

"But as for you, you meant evil against me; but God meant it for good, in order to bring it about as it is this day, to save many people alive" (Genesis 50:20).

Joseph never stopped believing God. He didn't know how to quit. He was sustained by the Word and by a God-given vision.

Detours didn't stop him. The road from the pasture to the palace was a long one. It was a perilous journey but by faith Joseph finished his course. At the end of the road, Joseph was able to look back and say, "God led me every step of the way. Even when the direction didn't make sense to me, God was in control. His goodness sustained me."

Disappointments didn't stop him. Have you ever been disappointed in someone? Have you ever been disappointed over the way someone treated you? Joseph's brothers threw him in a pit and then later sold him into slavery. Joseph's disappointment could have plunged him into discouragement and eventually despair, but faith sustained him. He got better, not bitter.

Delays didn't stop him. When the chief butler forgot to tell Pharaoh about his supernatural ability to interpret visions and dreams, Joseph served another two years in prison. That setback didn't rob him of faith. He grew stronger. Delays are difficult. Maybe you are discouraged today because you've waited a long time for a promise to be fulfilled, for a need to be met. Perhaps you've been walking through the "valley of the shadow of debt." It's easy to get discouraged in that valley, but don't do it. Listen to Joseph. He has something to say to you. So does the Apostle Paul:

"And let us not grow weary while doing good, for in due season we shall reap if we do not lose heart" (Galatians 6:9).

13

God Is Good All The Time

"Oh, how great is Your goodness, which You have laid up for those who fear You, which You have prepared for those who trust in You in the presence of the sons of men!" (Psalm 31:19)

God is good to those who fear Him—to those who boldly proclaim their trust in Him.

David was able to say "how great is Your goodness" even when in the natural, things weren't going so well. It is believed that he penned this psalm while being persecuted by Saul—hunted down like a criminal, living in caves like a fugitive.

The Psalm is a mixture of prayers, praises, and professions of confidence in God. David considered himself blessed because God was with him.

Consider the depth of his troubles:

"Have mercy upon me, O Lord, for I am in trouble: I am consumed with grief" (v. 9).

"I am forgotten as a dead man ... I am like a broken vessel" (v. 12).

"I have heard the slander of many: fear was on every side..." (v. 13).

Now consider David's secret of success and victory: His description of troubles was sandwiched between prayers, praises, and professions of faith.

"In Thee O Lord do I put my trust..." (v. 1).

"For You are my Rock and my Fortress..." (v. 3).

"...deliver me from the hand of my enemies..." (v. 15).

"Make Thy face to shine upon Thy servant: save me for Thy mercies sake" (v. 16).

"Be of good courage, and He shall strengthen your heart, all who hope in the Lord" (v. 24).

Troubles may be bad, but God is good. Why not join David in thanking and praising God for His goodness in the midst of your troubles. Anybody can praise Him after the troubles have passed. You are destined to triumph over trouble. Why? Because of the goodness of Your God.

14

God is Thinking about You

The Lord has been mindful of us."

Have you ever been tempted to think that God has forgotten you? He hasn't.

Did you ever feel as if you were all alone? You weren't.

"But Zion said, 'The Lord has forsaken me, and my Lord has forgotten me.' Can a woman forget her nursing child, that she should not have compassion on the son of her womb? Yes, they may forget, yet I will not forget you" (Isaiah 49:14-15).

God loves His children. You are in His heart and on His mind. In fact, He is thinking about you right now.

"For I know the thoughts that I think toward you, says the Lord, thoughts of peace (success and prosperity) and not of evil, to give you an expected end. (a future and a hope)" (Jeremiah 29:11).

In the hard times, when you're feeling down, remember the promise of a loving God, *"I will never leave you, nor forsake you" (Hebrews 13:5).*

You are not alone; you are never alone. Nor are you forgotten. God cares for you. You are in His heart and on His mind, His desire—His plan—is to bless and prosper you.

"The Lord has been mindful of us: He will bless us..." (Psalm 115:12).

15

God's Best

God intends to help us make the most of our lives. He is committed to help believers who seek and follow His will.

"I will instruct and guide you along the best pathway for your life; I will advise you and watch your progress" (Psalm 32:8 Living Bible).

God knows what is best for you. He wants what is best for you.

"For I know the thoughts that I think toward you, says the Lord, thoughts of peace and not of evil, to give you an expected end (a future and a hope)" (Jeremiah 29:11).

God's thoughts toward you—and His instructions to you—are contained in His Word. Learning, believing, and obeying the Bible is the pathway to God's best for your life.

"This Book of the Law shall not depart from your mouth, but you shall meditate in it day and night, that you may observe to do according to all that is written in it. For then you will make your way prosperous, and then you will have good success" (Joshua 1:8).

16

God's Kind Care

Annie Johnson Flint: <u>Suffering Saint</u>

Annie Johnson flint planned to become a concert pianist. But before her 20th birthday she was afflicted with crippling arthritis. Within five years she was hopelessly crippled, her hopes of being a concert pianist forever gone.

She could have become bitter and full of self pity but instead she chose another avenue of service. Her words of hope and faith have inspired thousands. Few people who read her beautiful writings realize that she wrote in

great pain, barely able to move a pencil. She
was laying flat on her back with a writing
board suspended above her when she wrote
these famous lines.

God's Kind Care

God hath not promised
Skies always blue,
Flower-strewn pathways,
All our lives thro';
God hath not promised
Sun without rain,
Joy without sorrow,
Peace without pain.

God hath not promised
We shall not know
Toil and temptation,
Trouble and woe;
He hath not told us
We shall not bear

Many a burden,

Many a care.

God hath not promised

Smooth roads and wide,

Swift, easy travel,

Needing no guide;

Never a mountain,

Rocky and steep,

Never a river

Turbid and deep.

But God hath promised

Strength for the day,

Rest for the labor,

Light for the way,

Grace for the trials,

Help from above,

Unfailing sympathy,

Undying love.

17

I Will Attack

my Lack

We have all experienced lack in some area of our lives at one time or another. We also know there is no lack in God. He is El-Shaddai, the all sufficient one, the God of plenty. He is more than enough.

There is a promise in God's Word to fit every need in our lives. There is provision in the promises.

The following steps from Oral Roberts have helped me a lot when I have been struggling with the discouragement that often accompanies lack. I hope they will bless you as they have me.

I Will Attack My Lack

1. I already have the faith I need to attack my lack.
2. I will start attacking my lack today.
3. My lack isn't beyond God's ability.
4. I can attack my lack through my giving and my receiving.
5. God has a personal harvest for me.
6. I will trust God as the Source of my Supply.
7. I will cheer up—roses will bloom again for me.
8. I will plant my best seeds.
9. I will pursue the God-kind of prosperity.
10. I am not out of options.
11. I will plant my seeds even during hard times.
12. I will use God's vocabulary.

18

The Pathway out

of Failure

Sow to yourselves in righteousness; Reap in mercy; Break up your fallow ground, For it is time to seek the Lord, Till He comes and rains righteousness on you" (Hosea 10:12).

Believers are to sow words and acts of righteousness. These words and acts are spiritual seeds which germinate in the soil of the heart, grow and eventually produce fruit. The type of fruit is determined by the type of seed.

Positive words planted in faith will result in a harvest of righteousness. Negative words planted in unbelief will result in a harvest of unrighteousness. It's that simple: you reap what you sow. Ultimately, the harvest you reap in life will be determined by the kinds of seeds you plant.

"Do not be deceived, God is not mocked; for whatever a man sows, that will he also reap" *(Galatian 6:7).*

The challenge is to speak positive words of faith when plagued with negative thoughts and feelings, or when surrounded by negative circumstances. Sowing negative words into an already negative situation certainly won't help. The pathway out of frustration and failure, and into faith and fulfillment, is paved with a mixture of positive thoughts, positive attitudes, and positive confessions.

What kind of harvest are you expecting? If you've been planting negative seeds, it's time to do some plowing. Break up your fallow ground and let righteousness soak into your soil. Then sow a different crop. You will be a lot more excited about the harvest to come.

19

Three Secrets of Success

1. Faith
2. Focus
3. Follow Through

<u>Faith</u> needs a vision to work toward. It needs a mountain to climb, a goal to pursue, a need to meet, a problem to solve. Faith wants to express itself in action.

<u>Focus</u>. Once faith goes to work on something focus is essential to success. Don't let

anything distract you. Keep your eyes on the prize.

"...let us run with endurance the race that is set before us. Looking unto (focusing on) Jesus, the author and finisher of our faith..." *(Hebrews 12:1-2).*

Follow Through. "Failure follows those who fail to follow through."

Stay positive and stay persistent. Watch out for the experts along the journey—the negative thinking experts who tell you it can't be done, you can't make it.

Declare *"I can do all things through Christ who strengthens me" (Philippians 4:13).*

Determine to, *"Press toward the mark for the prize of the high calling of God in Christ Jesus" (Philippians 3:14).*

If you begin with faith, stay focused, and follow through; you will achieve your goal.

20

God is Gracious

The friendship of the Lord is for those who fear Him, and He makes known to them His covenant. My eyes are ever toward the Lord, for He will pluck my feet out of the net. Turn thou to me, and be gracious to me; for I am lonely and afflicted" (Psalm 25:14-16).

David makes two general statements of faith in verse 14.

- The Lord befriends those who fear Him.
- He reveals His covenant to them.

He follows with a personal expression of faith in verse 15: *"I look to the Lord for I know He will deliver me."* He bases his prayer in verse 16 on the beliefs expressed in verses 14-15. *"Turn to me and be gracious to me for I am lonely and afflicted."*

I want you to notice several things here. First David honestly expressed his emotional pain to the Lord. *"I am lonely and afflicted"* (v. 16). In verse 17 and 18 he tells the Lord he is troubled and distressed.

Next I want you to notice that David kept his eyes on the Lord. He didn't get so focused on his troubles that he lost touch with God. *"My eyes are ever toward the Lord"* (v. 15).

Finally, I want you to see that David, though he was a great man of faith, had his share of problems and emotional struggles. But through it all, he maintained a positive attitude of faith. He never doubted God's friendship because he knew the strength of covenant. He knew it wasn't a question of "if" but "when" God would deliver him and be gracious unto him.

I think we should pray like David. Don't just say "God pluck my feet out of the net, help me, deliver me." But go on to pray with faith, "Lord turn to me and be gracious to me."

The Lord heard David's prayer and He will hear yours. God wants to do more than deliver you. He's not just your deliverer, He's your friend. He wants to be gracious unto you.

21

Attitude Determines Altitude

John 16:33 says, *"In the world you will have tribulation."* The second part gets better. Jesus said, *"But be of good cheer. I have overcome the world."*

Are you of good cheer today? You can be—even in the midst of the trial. Jesus overcame so you could be an overcomer.

You will always be faced with opposition. It's easy to drift downstream. It takes determination and effort to go upstream. The secret lies not only in overcoming the opposing forces, but in learning to use them to your advantage. That's right. You can actually learn to use them—some of them anyway—to your advantage.

Let me give you an example. How does an airplane get off the ground? It has to overcome the force of gravity. But not only does it overcome the force of gravity it uses this opposing force to produce lift. When I was in flight training I learned that to gain altitude the attitude of the plane had to be right. Attitude is a term used to describe the angle at which the plane is cutting through the air. That's why you hear me say periodically, "attitude determines altitude". How high do you want to get? How far do you want to go in God? You won't even get off the ground unless you get your attitude right.

Now, how do you use opposing forces to your advantage? By moving into them with the right attitude—a positive attitude of faith and victory.

Here's another example. In different times in my ministry people have come against me. There was opposition. I had to make a choice. Get angry and feel sorry for myself or forgive them and move on. I decided to get "better and not bitter". I decided to "be glad and not mad" (by the grace of God!) I decided to say, "It's joy unspeakable and full of glory," not "It's trials unbearable and full of misery".

What is the result today? I am blessed. I'm getting more blessed all the time. Some of the winds that came against me are blowing my direction now.

What's the key? The right attitude. The devil will try to put you under, but God will put you over. Jesus said, *"Be of good cheer. I have overcome the world."*

22

How to Overcome the Devil

And they overcame him because of the blood of the Lamb and because of the word of their testimony, and they did not love their life even when faced with death" (Revelation 12:11).

The legal basis for our spiritual authority is the blood of Jesus. Faith in the power of that blood gives us authority over the kingdom of darkness. The "testimony" of Revelation 12:11 is the evidence against Satan and his demons, the truth revealed and recorded in Scripture. It is a word spoken directly to our spiritual enemies: a word spoken in Jesus' name on the basis of His shed blood.

We must verbally assault the powers of darkness. We must boldly confront them with faith-filled testimony of the truth of God's word. We must plead the blood of Jesus; we must remind the powers of darkness that by faith in that blood we became God's property, and that they have no right to trespass. We must confront them with the truth that through the death of Christ they have been destroyed and that all their claims on us have been cancelled. We must proclaim their defeat and command them to depart in Jesus' name. There is power in a word spoken with legal force, with authority to back it up. The authority of heaven stands behind the words we speak in Jesus' name. That's why the devil hates to hear the testimony of a believer who knows the power of the shed blood of Jesus.

"Resist the devil and he will flee from you" (James 4:7).

23

Our Identity in Christ

I am complete in Him who is the head of all principality and power.
Colossians 2:10

I am victorious because *"greater is He who is in me than he who is in the world."*
1 John 4:4

I am the righteousness of God in Christ Jesus.
2 Corinthians 5:21

I am God's child for I am born again by the incorruptible seed of the word of God.

1 Peter 1:23

I am a new creation in Christ.

2 Corinthians 5:20

I am an heir of God in Christ.

Romans 8:17

24

New Hope for a New Age

We have hope for the future today because of the Resurrection of Jesus Christ from the dead. The person who does not know Jesus Christ as his Lord and Savior has no lasting hope for the future. The Bible teaches that before Jesus came we were, *"...without Christ, aliens from God's family and strangers from the covenants of promise, having no hope and without God in the world"* (Ephesians 2:12).

Faith in the Resurrection gives us hope of better things to come. The Resurrection helps us to look forward with certainty to the fulfillment of verses like Jeremiah 29:11, *"For I know the thoughts that I think toward you, says the Lord, thoughts of peace and not evil, to give you a future and a hope."*

"Behold I tell you a mystery; we shall not all sleep, but we shall all be changed—in a moment, in the twinkling of an eye, at the last trumpet. For the trumpet will sound and the dead will be raised incorruptible, and we shall be changed" (1 Corinthians 15:51-52).

25

By Faith and Force

"Blessed be the God and Father of our Lord Jesus Christ, who has blessed us with every spiritual blessing in the heavenly places in Christ...." (Ephesians 1:3).

Jesus redeemed you from the curse of the law and brought you under the blessing of the Covenant. The written Covenant was inspired by the Holy Spirit and sealed by the blood of Jesus. The Covenant blessings conveyed to believers are all recorded in God's word. Our part is to read, believe, claim, and, when necessary, take them from the devil.

God loves you. That is why He initiated a covenant and sealed it with the blood of His Son. God's desire is for you to experience the blessings of the Covenant. God doesn't withhold Covenant blessings from His children. We sometimes fail to experience them because of disobedience or unbelief, and, more often, because the powers of darkness get between us and the blessings sent our way by God. May God help us to zealously take by faith and force all that He has promised.

"Devil take your hands off what God has promised me. I bind your power in Jesus' name. I break your hold over the blessings sent my way by my Heavenly Father. Loose them and let them go in Jesus' name!"

"And from the days of John the Baptist until now the kingdom of heaven suffers violence,

and the violent take it by force." (Matthew 11:12).

It's legal to get violent with the powers of darkness which are working to hold back the Covenant blessings which are rightfully yours through faith in Jesus Christ. God has blessed you—past tense. It's already done. Now it remains for you and me to take from the devil by faith and force what God has promised.

26

The Secret of
the Lord

"The secret of the Lord is with those who fear Him, and He will show them His covenant" (Psalm 25:14).

God has promised blessing to those who keep His covenant—His word. Three blessings of Covenant relationship can be seen in Exodus 12 and 13. In these chapters God, in faithfulness to His covenant with Abraham, brings His covenant people out of Egyptian bondage. They are suddenly and dramatically brought out of bondage and into blessing

because God remembered—and was faithful—
to His covenant.

Covenant blessings we can see here are:

1. God's Protection

*"For the Lord will pass through to strike the
Egyptians; and when He sees the blood on the
lintel and on the two doorposts, the Lord will
pass over the door and not allow the destroyer
to come into your houses to strike
you"* (Exodus 12:23 see vs. 7-23).

2. God's Provision

*"Now the children of Israel had done according
to the word of Moses, and they had asked
from the Egyptians articles of silver, articles of
gold, and clothing. And the Lord had given the
people favor in the sight of the Egyptians, so
that they granted them what they requested.*

Thus they plundered the Egyptians" (Exodus 12:35-36).

3. God's Presence

"And the Lord went before them by day in a pillar of cloud to lead the way, and by night in a pillar of fire to give them light, so as to go by day and night. He did not take away the pillar of cloud by day or the pillar of fire by night from before the people" (Exodus 13:21-22 see vs. 17-22).

27

Winning in
the Wilderness

"So God led the people around by way of the wilderness of the Red Sea. And the children of Israel went up in orderly ranks out of the land of Egypt" (Exodus 13:18).

To believers, the "wilderness" is an experience, not just a place. Conversations with God's people in various parts of the country have convinced me that a lot of us are in the "wilderness." The Christian life is progressive—from "glory to glory" (2 Corinthians 3:18)—but that doesn't mean that you just make one quick trip through the "wilderness" and then remain forever in the "Promised Land."

I've been in and out of the wilderness several times in my walk with God. Sometimes my own mistakes have landed me back in the wilderness. When that happens, the best thing to do is get out as soon as possible in any way possible. There have been other times when God has led me into the wilderness (Matthew 4:1). When God leads us into the "wilderness" we shouldn't look for a way out. Rather, we should look for God in the wilderness. He may be doing a deep work in your heart that will count for eternity.

The "wilderness" (when God leads you into it) is meant to develop, not defeat, you. God's will is for you to win in the wilderness, to cope until you conquer.

We pass through many "wilderness" experiences: disappointment, death, emotional turmoil, waiting for an answer to prayer, darkness, etc. God's will is always for us to win in the "wilderness." Period.

So, don't make the mistake of always looking for a way out. Look for God and let Him develop you in your "wilderness" experience. The "wilderness" isn't so bad. Think of it. The children of Israel were supernaturally protected, directed, and provided for in the "wilderness." God performed miracle after miracle on their behalf. Yet, they complained constantly, yielded to unbelief, and disobeyed God.

There's a better way to travel through the wilderness—praising, believing, and obeying. The journey isn't so bad when you realize by faith what you have in the wilderness:

1. God's presence
2. God's power
3. God's provision
4. God's promise

Remember, you're just passing through. You're on the road to blessing and victory. And here's the best part—God is with you every step of the way.

"When you pass through the waters, I will be with you; and through the rivers, they shall not overflow you. When you walk through the fire, you shall not be burned, nor shall the flame scorch you" (Isaiah 43:2).

28

Don't Die in the Wilderness

God said something to Moses about the children of Israel in the wilderness that should arrest our attention.

"Say to them, 'Just as you have spoken in My hearing, so will I do to you'" (Numbers 14:28).

The first generation in the wilderness was apathetic, often discouraged, disobedient and short on faith. God heard daily complaints such as this: "It's too hard, we can't make it, why didn't Moses just leave us in Egypt, it was better there, and we're going to die in this wilderness." Their negative, unbelieving complaints became self destroying prophecies. They failed to enter the promised land and all but Joshua and Caleb (men of faith) died in the wilderness. God is merciful but He can't help His children who refuse to move out of unbelief into faith.

Paul says in Hebrews 3:16–4:2 that they failed to enter the promised land because of their disobedience and lack of faith. He issues a warning in Hebrews 3:12 which should be seriously heeded by every sincere believer in this apathetic generation.

"Beware, brethren, lest there be in any of you an evil heart of unbelief in departing from the living God" (Hebrews 3:12).

Anyone who understands the weight—and the consequences—of Paul's words in Hebrews 4:19 should immediately be done with apathy and careless Christian living:

"So we see that they could not enter in because of unbelief."

Is there faith in your heart today? If not, why not? If not, where can you find it? If not, what changes should you make in your life? Honestly attempting to answer these questions could mean the difference between perishing in the wilderness of unbelief or entering the promised land of faith.

29

Stake Your Claim

"*After the death of Moses the servant of the Lord, it came to pass that the Lord spoke to Joshua the son of Nun, Moses' assistant, saying: "Moses My servant is dead. Now therefore, arise, go over this Jordan, you and all this people, to the land which I am giving to them—the children of Israel. Every place that the sole of your foot will tread upon I have given you, as I said to Moses*" (Joshua 1:1-3).

The call in these verses is for aggressive action: to go forward to possess by faith what has been given. It is a call to rise up, invade enemy territory, and stake a claim on the basis of God's promises.

God's word to Joshua speaks to us today. *"Don't be discouraged. Don't be afraid. Move forward in faith. As I was with Moses, so I will be with you"* (Joshua 1:5-6, paraphrase).

The promise of God's presence and help gave Joshua confidence to stake his claim and press his claim. We have the same promise. The enemies say we can't have our promised inheritance; God says it's already ours by faith. The outcome is determined by who we agree with. Faith agrees with God, refutes the devil's lies, and takes hold of God's promises.

Whatever the present circumstances, we can expect success—if we:

1. Believe that God is with us
2. Obey His instructions

3. Claim and act on His promises

"This Book of the Law shall not depart from your mouth, but you shall meditate in it day and night, that you may observe to do according to all that is written in it. For then you will make your way prosperous, and then you will have good success" (Joshua 1:8).

30

The Foundation of Faith

Our faith is rooted in the Word of God.

"So then faith comes by hearing, and hearing by the word of God" (Romans 10:17).

We have faith in the Word of God because we know the faithfulness of the One who spoke the Word and inspired men to write it down. We have faith in the Word of God because, God stands behind His Word—watches over His Word to perform it.

"... there has not failed one word of all His good promise..." (1 Kings 8:56).

We can be "fully persuaded" because we trust in the faithfulness of God. Our faith is rooted in the Word of God. But the roots of our faith go even deeper—into the faithfulness of the One who spoke the Word. The Word is as good as the One who spoke it!

"And being 'fully persuaded' that what He had promised He was able also to perform" (Romans 4:21).

Why am I here? What is my purpose?

If you're like most people, you have a lot of questions you would like to have answered: Questions like, "Who am I?" "Why am I here?" "What does the future hold?" "What's life all about anyway?"

I used to ask the same questions. I often found myself sighing, "There's got to be more to life than this." There was an empty, unfulfilled feeling inside of me, a lonely ache in my heart. I tried just about everything to fill up that emptiness but nothing worked.

I was depressed, lonely, confused...and the merry-go-round I was riding on wouldn't stop to let me off! I was ready to give up on life. After trying everything I could think of there was still something missing. My life had no meaning. The emptiness was still there.

After trying everything else I turned to God for help. I was born again when I received Jesus as my Lord and Savior. He answered my questions. He filled the emptiness in my heart. He gave me peace, love and purpose in life. And I know He wants to do the same thing for you!

The Bible says that *"God loved the world so much that He gave His only begotten Son so that anyone who believes in Him shall not perish but have eternal life"* (John 3:16). Jesus said of Himself, *"I am the Way - yes, and the Truth and the Life, No one can come to the Father except by Me"* (John 14:6). He said, *"I have come that you might have life and have it abundantly"* (John 10:10).

I'm glad you decided to read this brief message. Now, my prayer is that you will do what I did - enter into a personal relationship with God by receiving Jesus Christ as your Savior.

There would never be a better time than right now to accept God's offer of love and forgiveness..."*For the wages of sin is death, but the gift of God is eternal life through Jesus Christ our Lord*" (Romans 6:23).

Have you decided to accept God's offer? Here's how to do it:

Believe on the Lord Jesus (Romans 10:9)

Repent or turn from the old way of life (Luke 13:3)

Confess your sins and ask God to forgive you (1 John 1:9)

Ask Jesus to save you (Romans 10:13)

If you are really sincere, say a prayer like this one:

God, I know I'm a sinner and I need forgiveness. I ask you to forgive my sins. Jesus, I open the door of my life to you and receive you as my Savior.

Are your sins really forgiven? Did Jesus really come into your life? Here's what the Bible says: *"If we confess our sins He forgives us and cleanses us from all unrighteousness"* (1 John 1:9). *"Behold I stand at the door and knock. If anyone opens the door I will come in"* (Revelation 3:20).

This is just the beginning of a new life for you! Try to find a good church, where you can share your experience with other Christians.